KITEBOARDING

BY JACK DAVID

BELLWETHER MEDIA • MINNEAPOLIS, MN

Are you ready to take it to the extreme?
Torque books thrust you into the action-packed world
of sports, vehicles, and adventure. These books may
include dirt, smoke, fire, and dangerous stunts.
WARNING: Read at your own risk.

This edition first published in 2009 by Bellwether Media.

No part of this publication may be reproduced in whole or in part without written permission of the publisher. For information regarding permission, write to Bellwether Media Inc., Attention: Permissions Department, Post Office Box 19349, Minneapolis, MN 55419.

Library of Congress Cataloging-in-Publication Data
David, Jack, 1968–
  Kiteboarding / by Jack David.
     p. cm. — (Torque : action sports)
  Summary: "Photographs of amazing feats accompany engaging information about Kiteboarding. The combination of high-interest subject matter and light text is intended for readers in grades 3 through 7"—Provided by publisher.
  Includes bibliographical references and index.
  ISBN-13: 978-1-60014-197-3 (hardcover : alk. paper)
  ISBN-10: 1-60014-197-8 (hardcover : alk. paper)
  1. Kite surfing—Juvenile literature. I. Title.

  GV840.K49D38 2009
  797.3—dc22   2008016609

CONTENTS

WHAT IS KITEBOARDING?

A gentle breeze pushes a huge, brightly colored kite through the air. In the water below, a rider on a board pulls back on the kite's ropes just as he hits a wave.

fast fact

Kiteboarding began on the East Coast of the United States in the late 1990s.

The rider launches into the air. He glides above the water for a few seconds before his board lands with a splash. It's the exciting sport of kiteboarding. It's one of the fastest-growing sports in the world.

Kiteboarding combines surfing, wakeboarding, and flying a kite. Kiteboarders use big, parachute-like kites to pull them over water, snow, ice, or even sand.

Sometimes they launch into the air for a short period of time. Kiteboarders don't need boats or planes or cars. All they need is their gear and some wind.

EQUIPMENT

The kite is the most important piece of kiteboarding gear. Kites are curved like parachutes to catch the wind.

Kiteboarders can choose from many different styles and sizes of kites. Popular styles include **foil kites** and **leading edge inflatable (LEI) kites**. Foil kites work best over ice and land. LEI kites are great for the water because they float.

Ropes attach the kite to a long bar called a **control bar**. The kiteboarder uses this bar to steer the kite. A **harness** secures the boarder to the control device. It gives support and keeps the boarder from losing his **rig**.

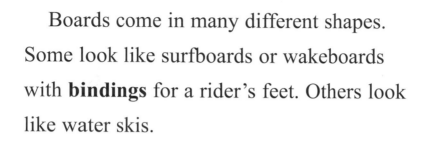

Boards come in many different shapes. Some look like surfboards or wakeboards with **bindings** for a rider's feet. Others look like water skis.

Fast Fact

Most kiteboarders like twin-tip boards. These boards don't have a set front or back.

On snow and ice, kiteboarders may use snowboards or skis. **Landboards** do well on dry surfaces such as sand and dirt.

KITEBOARDING IN ACTION

Kiteboarders can skim across waves or snow at 40 miles (64 kilometers) per hour or more. They can soar 30 feet (9 meters) into the air. They can perform spins, board **grabs**, and other tricks as they sail through the air.

A kiteboarder starts in a sitting or lying position. The boarder keeps the kite in a **neutral position**. This means that the kite is up in the air but isn't picking up the wind. Next, the boarder pulls the control bar so that the kite moves to catch the wind. The kite pulls the boarder up on top of the water or in to a standing position on the ground. The kiteboarder uses the control bar to turn and jump, and to bring the kite down to end the run.

Some kiteboarders take part in competitions. They perform in front of judges. The judges score kiteboarders on their jumps and tricks.

The kiteboarder with the highest jumps and best tricks wins the event. Competitions are a great place to see the world's best kiteboarders show off their skills.

GLOSSARY

binding—a set of straps that keep a boarder's feet attached to the board

control bar—a bar attached to a kite by long lines which allows a boarder to control the kite

foil kite—an arc-shaped kite made of a material such as nylon; foil kites have air cells through which air flows to inflate the kite; they are best suited for use on land and snow.

grab—a trick in which a kiteboarder grabs the board while in the air

harness—a set of straps that supports a boarder and is secured to the control device

landboard—kiteboards used on land; landboards do not have fins.

leading edge inflatable (LEI) kite—a popular kind of kite that includes inflatable compartments that give the kite its shape and help it float

neutral position—the position in which a kiteboarder holds the kite before starting a run; the kite is in the air but isn't pointed directly into the wind.

rig—the name for a full set of kiteboarding equipment

TO LEARN MORE

AT THE LIBRARY

Holzhall, John. *Secrets of Kiteboarding*. Paia, Hawaii: KiteBoard Center LLC, 2004.

Preszler, Eric. *Kiteboarding*. Mankato, Minn.: Capstone, 2005.

Woods, Bob. *Water Sports*. Milwaukee, Wisc.: Gareth Stevens, 2004.

ON THE WEB

Learning more about kiteboarding is as easy as 1, 2, 3.

1. Go to www.factsurfer.com
2. Enter "kiteboarding" into search box.
3. Click the "Surf" button and you will see a list of related web sites.

With factsurfer.com, finding more information is just a click away.

INDEX